Jono's
Rescue

Story by Chris Bell
Illustrations '

PM Plus Chapter Books

Sapphire

U.S. Edition © 2004 Harcourt Achieve Inc.
10801 N. MoPac Expressway
Building #3
Austin, TX 78759
www.harcourtachieve.com

Text © 2004 Chris Bell
Illustrations © 2004 Cengage Learning Australia Pty Limited
Originally published in Australia by Cengage Learning Australia

10 11 12 13 14   1957   15 14 13 12 11
4500273154

Text: Chris Bell
Printed in China by 1010 Printing International Ltd

Jono's Rescue
ISBN 978 0 75 786932 7

Contents

Chapter One
Free to a Good Home

"Hey, kid. You want some kittens?"

Jono stared up at the older boy blocking his path.

"I've got some of them here. They're free. I have to get rid of them."

Jono shook his head. His mom was allergic to cats. She couldn't even be in the same room with them. Besides, he was hopelessly late for swimming practice, and Coach would make him do an extra 20 laps as punishment.

"No, sorry. I can't," he answered, frowning anxiously at his watch.

Jono broke into a run. The boy wouldn't harm them, would he?

Against the glare of the setting sun, Jono turned back and saw the silhouette of a figure, arm raised, standing on the wall by the river. His heart skipped a beat. As if in slow motion, he watched the figure release something from his hand. Jono was already running back before the bag hit the water. He knew exactly what was in it.

Jono's heart pounded and his stomach hurt as he raced back along the path and headed for the grassy strip that ran alongside the water's edge.

The bag hit the surging water with a splash, and was swept swiftly downstream. His only hope of catching it now was to swim for it.

He tore off his shoes and watch, and stripped to his shorts. He stared down at the swirling brown water, took a deep breath, and plunged in before he could change his mind.

Icy water swirled around him, and Jono gasped in shock. He propelled himself upward, struggling to keep his head above the gushing current.

The sack was barely visible ahead of him. It was in quieter water now, bobbing up and down as it drifted along. Jono wondered if the kittens would survive by the time he caught up. Could they swim inside the bag? He had no way of knowing, but he had to try to rescue them — no matter what!

Jono battled the foaming water, which filled his eyes and nostrils, and threatened to pull him down to its dangerous depths. One frantic stroke followed another, until gradually the water grew calmer and he neared the bag. For a moment, it snagged on a fallen branch and he gained valuable seconds.

He lunged forward. In two more strokes, his hand closed around the bag and he forced it above the surface. He treaded water for a moment, and then headed for the riverbank.

He collapsed onto the shore, panting for breath. Then he quickly untied the bag and opened it, afraid of what he might find.

Chapter Two
What to Do Now?

One by one, Jono pulled out five, tattered, shivering balls. They were tiny and soaked — but they were alive!

His relief was short-lived.

What was he going to do now? There was no way he could take the kittens home. Then he had a thought. If the cats were small, wouldn't Mom be less allergic? He didn't know. He only knew he had a real problem. In fact, looking at the tiny, frightened bundles, he now had five problems.

In the winter twilight, Jono hurried back to where he'd left his things. He checked his watch. There wasn't much point in going to practice now. With teeth chattering, he quickly dressed, and then used his towel to rub each little kitten dry.

Whenever he put one down, it raced off toward the water's edge. Before long, Jono was scurrying in all directions trying to scoop up kittens, until finally he spied his bag. "Sorry guys. You'll have to go in here until I figure out what to do."

Mom and Abby, his younger sister, would pick him up from the pool at 6:30, which meant Jono had just one hour to find homes for five kittens.

He walked up and down the main street near the pool. The stores were closing, and no one wanted to stop.

He saw a young woman and held out an appealing orange and white fluffball. "I'd love to take her home," she said, "but I can't really afford to feed another cat."

Jono reached into his pocket and drew out his only money. "I'll throw in five dollars for food," he pleaded, then sighed with relief as she smiled and took the kitten. He was poorer, but at least he only had four kittens left.

It was twenty past six. He just had time to make it to the pool.

The journey home seemed neverending. Jono coughed and spluttered the entire way, to hide the faint but unmistakeable meowing coming from his bag.

His mother fussed. "You'll catch pneumonia swimming in this weather!" she said.

Jono nearly choked. Imagine if she knew where he'd really been swimming!

He considered telling Mom the truth, but there never seemed to be the right moment. He studied her face out of the corner of his eye. So far, she showed no symptoms or reaction — no sneezes, red lumps, or rash.

"Why do you keep looking at me?" she asked. "Have I got something awful on my face?"

Jono glanced away. Not yet, he thought.

When they arrived home, Mom said, "You might as well give me your swim suit. I'm doing laundry."

"Oh, no," said Jono quickly. "I'll do it, Mom. You always say I should wash my own stuff."

"Okay," she said in surprise, looking puzzled as she walked away.

Phew, that was close.

"Achoo!" A loud sneeze echoed from the kitchen, followed by another and another.

Uh-oh, thought Jono. Here it comes!

Chapter Three
Somewhere to Hide

Jono grabbed his bag and fled to his room. He searched around for somewhere to hide the kittens, but the only place he could think of was in his laundry basket.

By now the kittens were meowing furiously. They must be hungry, he thought, but what do they eat? Milk? Ordinary cat food? Or was there special kitten food?

He jumped guiltily as footsteps tapped down the hall. He only just slammed shut the lid on the basket when Mom walked into the room.

Jono's eyes widened in horror. Draped around her neck was his towel. She pulled it off and shook it at him angrily. "This was on the laundry floor. Is the rest of your stuff in the wash?"

Jono nodded dumbly. He stared at Mom's neck, which was covered in angry red welts.

"Achoo!" she sneezed. "Must be hayfever weather. I haven't felt like this since Abby brought home that stray cat."

Jono stopped breathing for a second, but Mom went away, blowing her nose.

This is serious, he thought. There must be somewhere he could hide the kittens that Mom wouldn't go.

15

Finally Jono thought of just the right hiding spot — Mom's knitting basket! It was stored under the stairs, abandoned since Mom's last disastrous attempt at knitting a sweater for him.

That night, when Mom and Abby were asleep, Jono crept into the hall. No one ever ventured under the stairs, except to store things.

Too late, he remembered the horrible squeak of the stairwell door. The sound pierced the quiet darkness.

Nothing moved. Even the kittens stayed silent. Jono breathed again.

He left them, whispering, "Behave yourselves. I'll be back in the morning."

Early the next morning, Mom drove Jono to swim practice. By the time he'd swum Coach's extra laps and walked home, Mom and Abby had gone shopping. That gave Jono a chance to feed the kittens and give them some run-around time.

When he heard the car pull into the driveway, Jono quickly placed the kittens back into the basket under the stairs. When Mom and Abby walked in he was leaning against the stairwell door.

Mom's neck appeared nearly normal now. Only a faint redness gave away her near encounter with the kittens. "Would you move, please, Jono?"

"W... What?" he stammered.

"Move, please! I bought some new yarn and I want to get my knitting basket."

Jono's eyes widened. "N... n... now?"

"MOVE," said Abby loudly.

Jono had gained valuable thinking time. "I'll get it, Mom. You go and have a cup of coffee. I'll bring the basket."

Mom looked at him suspiciously. "Okay, but you're acting very strangely, young man. I suspect you're up to something."

Jono had to move fast. He snatched up the kittens and raced to his room. He had no choice now but to hide them back in the laundry basket.

It took some smooth talking to convince Mom that everything was all right, but eventually she seemed satisfied. Jono returned to his room and collapsed on his bed. Sharp meows came from the basket. These kittens were more demanding than Coach!

Jono yanked off the lid of the basket. "Now listen you ... three?"

Uh-oh! Three? There should be four! Keep calm, Jono told himself. He yanked out T-shirts and pajamas from the basket. There was no fourth kitten to be found.

He checked under the bed, in his closet, and in every nook and cranny.

No fourth kitten!

Jono crawled along the hall, whispering, "Here, kitty, kitty, kitty."

As he passed Abby's room, he heard her having a tea party with a friend. "Would you like one lump of sugar or two?"

Friend? What friend? Silently he opened her door. There was Abby offering a cup of tea to a snowy white kitten wearing a curly-haired wig.

"What are you doing?" Jono hissed.

"Look what I found!" Abby giggled with delight.

"You didn't find it. It's mine."

"Does Mom know?" shrieked Abby, wide-eyed.

"Sshhhh!"

Abby began to cry, and Jono had to negotiate fast. When he walked out of the room, he couldn't believe the promise he'd made. Nothing was worth that. Nothing!

Chapter Four
Allergic to Jono?

With the kitten safely stowed back in his room, Jono went to the kitchen for a drink.

Mom sat at the table sorting out her yarn, her knitting basket by her side. Her face was swelling into welts.

"Achoo!"

Mom looked up worriedly. "Oh, Jono. I didn't see you. How long have you been standing there?"

"Not long," answered Jono.

"I'm starting to worry," said Mom in a small voice. "Jono, I think I'm becoming allergic to you!"

Jono choked on his juice. "No," he spluttered. "You're not allergic to me. It probably is the weather."

Mom scratched quickly at her cheek and down her neck. "No, I don't think so, but something very weird is happening. Every time I'm in the same room as you, I start to sneeze, scratch, or itch."

"Oh, Mom, it's just your imagination."

He hurried back to his room with his fingers crossed behind his back.

Right after lunch, Jono called to Mom from the porch, "I'm just going next door to see Peter."

"Don't be long," she replied.

He shut the front door and tucked a kitten further up his sweater. His neighbor already had two dogs, a rabbit, a chicken, two mice, and a bowl of fish. Surely one more pet wouldn't matter!

But for once, it seemed as though Mrs. Meade was going to say no. But then Jono pulled out the tabby fluffball with big velvet eyes, and with one look at Peter's mom's face, Jono knew she'd say yes.

Hooray! Only three more to go. This wasn't so hard after all.

It took the entire afternoon for Jono to telephone every person he knew. By nightfall he had only one kitten left — one little black cat with a crooked eye.

Jono stroked her soft fur and promised he'd find her a good home. Then Mom knocked on his door, and he shoved the kitten underneath his pillow.

"I've been calling and calling you. Come and eat your dinner, now."

Jono leaped off the bed and followed Mom out.

Dinner was torture!

Jono sat opposite Mom, and every time he glanced at her, she looked back suspiciously. Every few seconds, she'd scratch furiously at her face and neck and then peer at him.

When she sneezed out a mouthful of peas, Jono could hardly even laugh. Well, not as hard as he normally would have, anyway.

Chapter Five
The Worst Punishment

After dinner Jono suggested that he make a fire and they toast marshmallows.

"And I'll knit by the fire," said Mom. "I haven't done that for ages."

Jono went into the living room to start the fire. *Meow.*

Jono continued to stack the logs. "Now I'm imagining I hear cats," he muttered.

Meow. Oh, no! That was no imaginary cat. The meow had come from the chimney. It couldn't be. Could it?

"Are you ready?" called Mom from the kitchen. "I've got the marshmallows."

"Nearly," yelled Jono, thinking fast. The kitten must have escaped from his bedroom. Perhaps he hadn't closed the door all the way. But how could the kitten have climbed up the chimney? He could hear Mom in the kitchen. She'd be in any second.

No time to lose. Jono crouched down in the fireplace and nervously thrust his head up inside the chimney.

He breathed in a mouthful of soot. Yuck! He could just make out two little eyes looking back from a ledge in the chimney.

"Jono! What are you doing?"

"Ouch!" Jono's head smacked against the chimney wall as Mom's voice echoed in his ears. He pulled back out of the chimney, dripping soot onto the hearth.

"Come out of there," said Mom. "Look at the mess you've made."

Jono climbed out of the fireplace and stood, soot-faced and red-eyed.

Things just kept getting worse, no matter what he did.

He didn't see Mom pick up a box of matches from the mantel. But suddenly he heard the strike of a match.

"No, Mom! Stop!"

"Whatever is the matter, Jono? I'm just lighting the fire."

Jono blew frantically, trying to stop the wood from catching fire.

"Enough," snapped his mother. "What's going on?"

The game was up. Jono had no choice but to tell Mom everything — about missing practice, the boy with the cats, the half-drowned kittens, and how he'd tried to find homes for them all.

When he finished, Mom shook her head. "I do understand, Jono. But I'm still angry with you. This will mean losing a week's allowance. If you had told me sooner, we could have called the animal shelter."

"Well, there is one good thing," mumbled Jono. "At least you're not allergic to me."

Mom pursed her lips. "Achoo!" she sneezed. "Get that cat out of here!"

Jono took the last kitten next door to Peter's. Mrs. Meade would take care of it until another home was found. Maybe she'd even feel sorry for the little black cat with the crooked eye and adopt it, too.

But the kitten wasn't Jono's biggest problem.

In 24 hours, he'd missed practice, and had to swim an extra 20 laps. He'd nearly drowned and almost caught pneumonia, and now he'd lost a week's allowance!

But that wasn't the worst part. As Jono opened the front door, more punishment awaited.

There was Abby, standing against the wall, grinning and holding her doll's tea set ... and a curly-haired wig.

Rigby PM Plus Chapter Books

Level 29

25
26
27
28 29
30

Jono's Rescue

Jono saves some kittens from drowning in a river, but what will he do with them? His mom is allergic to cats, and no one else seems to want them. He tries hiding them at home, but Mom is starting to sneeze. Jono needs to find homes for the kittens, fast!

RIGBY
PM
Plus

ISBN 0-7578-

9 780757 869327

ISBN 0 75786 932 7

W7-BMO-817

Brave One

Story by Julie Mitchell

Illustrations by Elise Hurst